The alkalinity of bottled water

Makhosazana Xaba

Published by Botsotso in 2019

Box 30952
Braamfontein 2017

botsotso@artslink.co.za
www.botsotso.org.za

ISBN 978-0-9947081-6-8

The poems©Makhosazana Xaba

Editor: Allan Kolski Horwitz
Layout, design and cover: Vivienne Preston

Tomorrow awaits our awakening.

The reconstructed us.
The self-conscious collective.
The responsible & inspired us.

Tomorrow will not abandon us.

Contents

Part 3

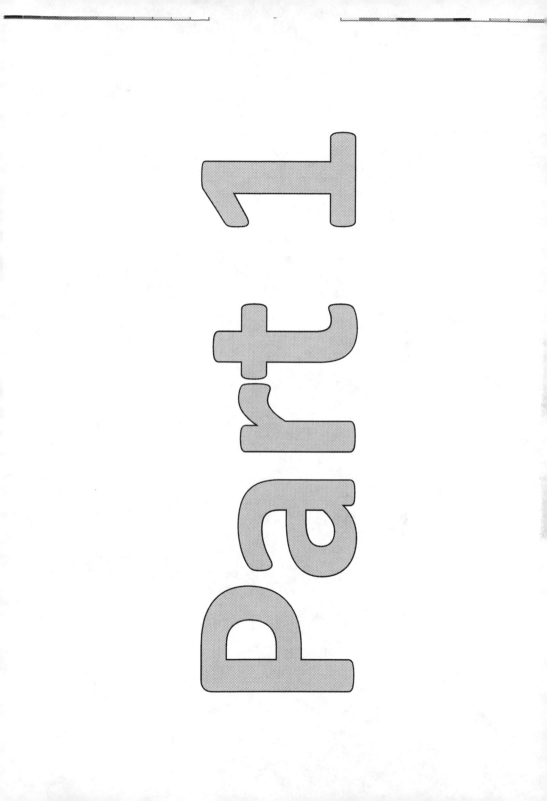

Part 1

When laughter hurts

When laughter hurts, something breaks
Pieces fly in the air, cutting into anything and anyone
On their corridor of flight
But somewhere, some bleed

When laughter hurts and some bleed
The smell of fresh blood nauseates
Though others bleed in solidarity
Despite the choke, despite the vomit

When laughter hurts and others vomit
Contamination spreads
The atmosphere turns foul
And so, in time, we marinate in the affliction

The nation was preoccupied

How shall we remember this time, when
the nation was preoccupied with one man's appointments?

How shall we remember this time, when
the nation was preoccupied with one man's charges?

How shall we remember this time, when
the nation was preoccupied with one man's home?

How shall we remember this time, when
the nation was preoccupied with one man's laughter?

How shall we remember this time, when
The nation was preoccupied with one man's penis?

These four words

It is time to go to bed so I must summon stillness,
silence the voices, erase the visuals, concentrate.

But first, I will complete my evening routine:
turn off the geyser;
boil water and soak slices of limes and lemons;
brush my teeth;
read messages and respond to deserving ones;
set the alarm for 04:30;
pack the yoga bag and place it next to the back door;
lock all the doors;
turn on the wall lights facing the street;
double-check the two main doors are locked.

And all the while, these words –
Bright red, repeating,
Disrupting like thunder,
Promising like stars shining through the dark night sky –
These four words live in my head:

Pay back the Money!

Goodbye my lake

The Ugandans knew you as Nalubaale.
The arrivals renamed you, Lake Victoria.
And I, I called you, my lake.

You and I first met nineteen years ago,
A week before we, South Africans, immersed
Our beings in the magic of our dreams.
When you and I spoke, I shared my anxieties,
Those at the core of my exhilarating anticipation.
You told me: all would be well.

Today, a few months before we celebrate
Two decades of democracy, I don't want to go back home
Because all is not well and you know it.

Nineteen years ago you and I spoke from Jinja.
Today we speak from Entebbe. If you were a river
I would jump into you, so I could flow with you,
Float as my back rests on you and my eyes take in the sky.

In time, we would be at one with the Nile.
And at that point I would swim northwards,
Gesture a goodbye to southern-ness,
Give northern-ness a nod as I arrive at the sea.

With arms in the air, I would give my body to the Mediterranean.
But for now home beckons and duty calls my name.

Goodbye, my lake.

The alkalinity of bottled water

My subject: On the Comparisons of Alkalinity Levels in Bottled Water
In the distance, I hear the now familiar song: *Solomoni! Iyo Solomoni!*
Peering through the buildings of Braamfontein, unaltered by the strong winds,
From the window of our 7th floor office, we saw the shooting of a Catholic priest.

The milliequivalents per litre (mVal) of water, commonly known as the pH
Did these jacaranda trees ever imagine a sight like this? In front of the Wits Great Hall:
Many police vans, black men in uniform stand with guns in their hands
Facing a handful of students, singing and unarmed.

This poem on the alkalinity of bottled water veers to the water we are sinking into
Parents have not forgotten the words of the minister of higher education;
The words he uttered & then laughed: "Students Must Fall!" I hear the sounds of
Struggle: Siyaya! Siyaya! These Wits students have not fallen. Not now.

The pH of this water must rise because that is how the body detoxifies
As the ire of students rises throughout the country, as universities burn,
As the minister of finance prepares for his budget speech, as he receives charges
From the NPA – the rand falls; anxieties about relegation to junk status rise.

The mVal of water we have sunk into is falling & we have forgotten that
The CEO of the SABC returned to his job. The news of raging fires, of burning books!
The end of the seven-year term of the first woman Public Protector this country has
known, is here.
The report on state capture is looking for a safe place, has had to wait for court
judgement.

As we waver in this water, as we discuss the dangers of this descent
We reach to our inner core for the power we once possessed, the power
We once knew we had, in a time we once owned, when the line was indelible.
We now need an end to the welcome disruptions. We welcome the incoming Public
Protector.

While working on this poem, I take a call from a literary scholar who tells me:
"Apologies the poetry session has been cancelled, no visitors allowed at the University of Pretoria."
During this period of flaring fires, rising students & conversations about decolonizing:
Shaeera Kalla. Bullets on your back. Fezekile Ntsukela Kuzwayo. Ten years later, we look back.

This poem has settled with the analysis of the alkalinity of the water we are drowning in
As our arms flail in desperation, we hope to start seeing a hard rock below,
Waiting at the unfathomable bottom. Fezekile, the four sisters ensured
That we never forget: Kufezekile! And for that, the pH rises and we with it.

As the rock becomes visible, we strengthen our arms & legs, some pray, others sing
We dive with smiles on our faces because we realize that the turning point is close.
We would be singing out loud if we were not under water, so we focus on not drowning
So that we can rise again, resurface and realize the dreams of the democracy we want.

20 October 2016

The sky agrees

They understand our sorrows, imbibe our stories.
They carry our memories and create their own.
They articulate philosophies and choose fitting actions.
They show us our shortcomings.

Though they feel deceived, they stand up and speak out,
Demand and proclaim, occupy.
They study while sitting; tweet, post,
Broadcast the revolution.

They have changed the new we thought we had created.
Even the sky agrees – the beautiful ones have arrived.

Tentacles

The tentacles of white men in academia
Go deep, spread wide, entangle,
Cross time.

Says a Black woman scholar,
The only solution is to wait
...
...
...
...
...
...
...
...
...
...
...
...
...
...
...
...
...
...
...
...
...
...
...
...
...
...
...
...
for them to die.

The phantom shebeen

The well-known Saxonwold suburb
Has a phantom shebeen.

Some say it's a shebeen where people
Gather for a special communal shedding of tears.

Others say it's an underground shebeen into which
People disappear to hold secret meetings.

Some agree it's an underground shebeen
But they say it is sacred ground for coal mines.

Others posit it's a hypothetical shebeen –
A tactical decoy for transactional deeds.

Some even call it by name: The Sax Tender Tavern,
A secret and savvy sojourn for the larneed elite.

Some declare there is no shebeen in Saxonwold –
A "pub" or a "saloon", maybe, but not a shebeen!

Now driving and walking this suburb has changed forever.
And I walk its streets with a storybook stride.

That weekend in December

That weekend in December was too short.

There was no time to change
The photograph on the wall because
Ministerial show pieces call for considered curating.

That weekend in December was too long
Because billions of rands evaporated.

[1]*In December 2015 the then President Zuma replaced Finance Minister Nhlanhla Nene with David "Des" Van Rooyen whom he soon replaced with Pravin Gordhan*

The storytelling jug

I am the two litre jug, plastic and royal blue.
I was brought to this home as a gift five years ago.
The first born daughter of the Mother of this home
Used her first salary to buy her mother a special gift.
"Mama you need a decent dedicated kitchen jug" she said.

The daughter, Sozesazi, had a smile of pride when she presented me;
Until then I had been living for years at Vukani General Dealers.
No one wanted me. I had learned to love the smell of dust.
I learned to listen to voices of shoppers and relished their touch.
"What do you think of this one? Too blue, maybe," they said.

Then one day, when the Mother and Father of this home
Were sleeping in their bedroom, a boy I had never seen
Stormed into the kitchen, filled me up with tap water,
Walked down the corridor into the main bedroom.
"Here, wash her with this," and handed me to another boy.

This boy was naked on top of the Mother of the home.
With speed he shifted, emptied me of the water
Down the legs of the Mother of this home, then threw
Me on the floor where the father of the home was kneeling.
"Help me. Help us. Please!" his eyes and face were saying.

Large brown tape covered his mouth, his hands were tied behind.
He rocked from side to side – I thought
It was his way of comforting himself. Then I counted
Five boys in the bedroom, one was emptying the drawers.
"It's your turn, go fill up the jug!" he screamed, pointing at another.

I was back in the kitchen, in the hands of another boy
Who did what the other boy had done but didn't close the tap.
Back in the bedroom, I was aware of the dripping water, I knew
That the Mother of this home would hate that. One boy got off her.
"You took all the juices, she's dry!" He sounded angry.

They must have rehearsed this going to the kitchen part.
The climbing on the bed, moving up and down the Mother,
The moaning each climber emitted before getting off the bed.
I had seen many things in this home and at the General Dealers.
"Hurry up Magents, its getting dark outside!" one of them said.

And so finally they had to stop taking turns with the Mother of the home.
When they left they were running, all five of them. The Mother of the
Home removed the tape from her mouth and started crying so loud
I thought the ceiling would crack. Very slowly she moved and climbed down.
"I am coming Baba. Let me get a pair of scissors," all this time she was crying.

The Mother and the Father of this house left on that day.
I decided I would become the storytelling jug from then on.
Always, I start with the words, "I am the two litre jug; plastic and royal blue.
I came to this home a gift of a daughter to her mother, many years ago."
Then I tell the story in a manner that matches my mood on the day.

On some days I focus on the silences between sounds that filled this house.
On other days I give life to their words because I remember them all.
On most days I tell the story just the way it unfolded, on that yesterday-like day.
I was once a dedicated kitchen jug. I evolved into a storytelling jug:
Decent, two litres in volume, plastic and royal blue.

Ten years later

In a time as momentous as
An eclipse of the moon,
They stand in public view.

As we witness the confrontation,
We hear the eloquence of their silence
Touch their presence.

The placards speak:

> **Remember Khwezi**
> **I am I in 3**
> **Khanga**
> **Ten years later**

Dressed in black, each body frames each message.

Our tears and smiles harmonise;
We stroke our goose bumps.

Four women speak for millions.

Home address

She refuses to pack and leave.
Every morning she prays out loud – twice – while
Standing in front of the massive wooden door,
Kneeling for the third time in front of the eternal flame.

She tells them the flame is her own fire,
That she cooks her meals there, and sleeps there on cold nights;
That she taught herself to read by standing in front of the lettered door.
She tells them the colossal door is a superwoman.

When they say she has lost her mind,
She says that is a lie.
Her home address is: "Hilltop"
And her name is Dedani.

Twenty-one houses

The reporters said all the houses were empty and dirty.
We heard laughter in both bedrooms of the first house;
We listened to its rhythm & counted the cadences,
Measured its volume. It was pure, unmistakable laughter.

The journalists said all the houses were unoccupied and filthy.
We saw lies in both bedrooms of the second house:
Lies packed on shelves along the walls, neat and dust free; like books,
They rested these lies, looking at home, unbothered; unwilling to move.

The reporters said all the houses were dirty and empty.
At first we thought it was paint decorations. Then we smelled it: blood.
Jelly-like blood splattered on walls, windows and the floor;
Blinding and dizzying blood in this third house made all of us sick.

The journalists said all the houses were filthy and unoccupied.
We saw things falling from the roof of the fourth house:
Things without shape, without names, things dislocating, dropping.
We looked up and ducked. The roof could not contain the falling.

The reporters said things about the houses we could not confirm.
When we opened the door of the fifth house water hit us
Flood-like determined to evict us. At first we walked backwards
Then we turned around and ran. Water in the year of drought!

The 2016 Coffin

Inside the coffin, a black man.
Outside the coffin, two white men,
Two flying threats: petrol and a snake.

On the witness stand, two white men.
Outside the court, people united in protest.
The memory of this coffin: alive in our muscles.

---

[2] *The incident became known as the "coffin case". Willem Oosthuizen and Theo Jackson assaulted and put Victor Mlotshwa in a coffin in August 2016 after accusing him of stealing. They were later sentenced to 11 and 14 years in jail, respectively for attempted murder.*

Forget about apartheid?

Tell that to the young people shouting: Bring back our land!
They carry intergenerational stories of mass removals
Under their skins where memories crawl like worms . . . lingering.

Tell that to the woman whose son was last seen thirty years ago
Inside an inyala van driven by a white man in a SADF uniform;
This woman who attends all exhumations she ever hears about . . . hoping.

Tell that to the three sisters whose parents died in exile before
They returned to fetch them. All three vowed never to have their own children,
In case they too never know their parents' loving.

Tell that to this sixty-year-old woman, raped and tortured in prison
Whose scars from the torture rods of metal never left her thighs,
Who disallowed herself the freedom of nudity, even after the TRC & its
"forgivings".

Tell that to that octogenarian on a wheelchair (once a young lion)
When the voices of his grandchildren ring in his head:

> *But grandpa you never want to tell me who took your legs away?*
> *Grandpa where can I get my own wheelchair? I want to be like you.*
> *Why you don't have legs grandpa? Mama said I must ask you.*
> *Grandpa don't you have a speedometer in your wheelchair?*
> *I can go looking for your legs grandpa, I am good at finding things.*

Forget about apartheid?

Friends?

She is my friend. No, she was my friend —
Over time, we went our separate ways.

She became richer when her father died;
I became poorer when my parents retired.

When she moved to the coast, another inconvenience:
The distance between our homes.

When she visits the city, she worries about the safety of her car
outside my home.
When I travel for work not too far from the coast, I cannot afford
to travel to hers.

Although we still chat, the content builds walls between us;
Her holidays longer, the number of her white friends larger.

Although she still plans on learning an indigenous language,
I – her preferred practice ground – have become an absence.

She was my friend when we were anti-apartheid activists.
What are we today? The common enemy has yet to surface.

Our hill

On top of this hill sits our conscience.

Inside the belly of this hill
Rest our stories.

Winds blow around this hill,
Keeping it in check and intact –
Carving a monument of our oneness.

The eyes of the world scrutinise this hill.
The feet of the world walk this hill.

In the privacy of our individual selves,
I believe, we honour this, Our Hill.

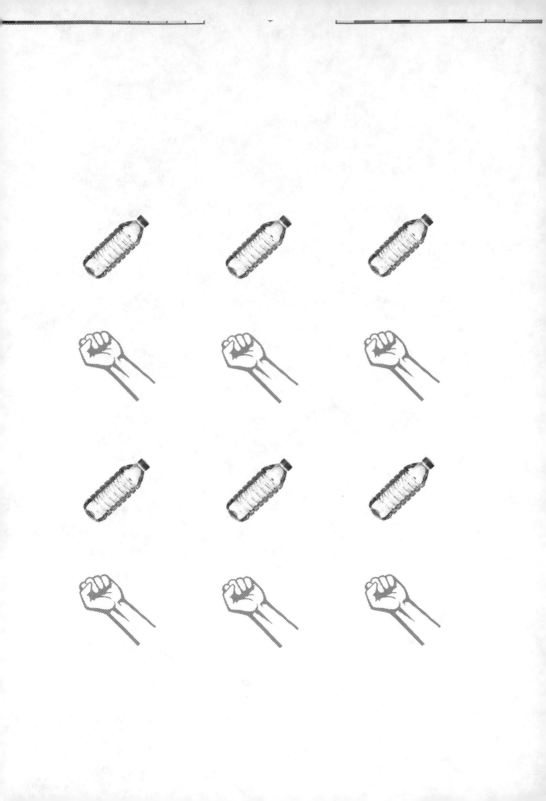

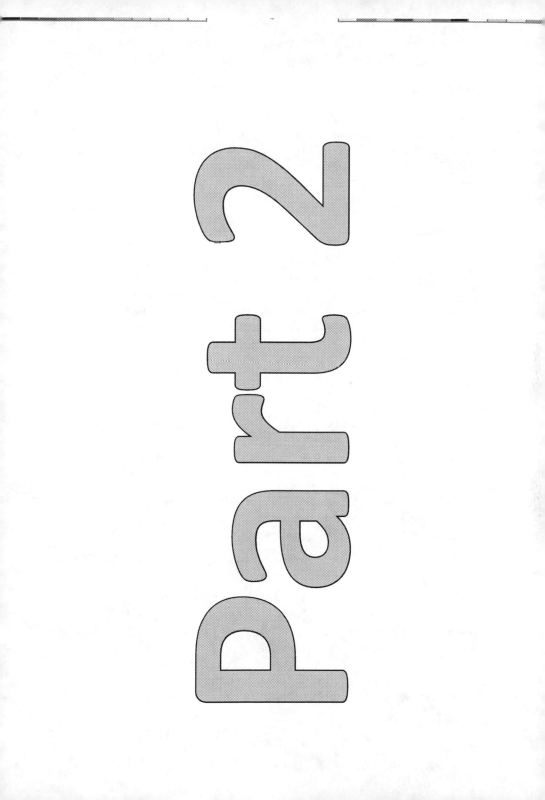

Part 2

Welcome

Welcome to our kitchen.
Everything in here is old, bar the fridge and the microwave
but the food is served fresh to massage the mouth. It feeds the soul
unlike the one at the Mapungubwe hotel in the Joburg CBD –
the one in which you did not offer me coffee or tea
and instead asked me to get comfortable on the bed while promising:
I will not do anything you don't want me to do.
The kitchen needs a new and modern look; I hope you will find some nurturing it in.

Say hello to my bedroom.
Pictures of my sisters, my daughter and my mother live here, in their frames
because this room is my private room, my haven. It houses my heart.
This queen size bed – unlike one at the Southern Sun hotel, O.R. Tambo airport –
isn't king size, we cannot cuddle across its width but, there's an electric blanket
you won't have to remind me in that child-like tone:
Oh, I can't stand this weather, Durban is so much warmer!
It needs de-cluttering and order; may it give you nights full of ever-sweet dreams.

And this, this is our lounge.
Salute the wall hangings: the wooden comb from Zambia, the beaded Masai necklace,
these clocks of Namibian rock, the women figurines of Zimbabwean soap stone.
This lounge – unlike the lounge of your room at the Protea hotel, Wanderers –
is without a view, the view from where you stood waiting for me to arrive
in the blue Mazda, the car I heard you mention matter-of-factly to the receptionist:
See that car, that deep blue car over there? It is now my home.
Memories of laughter live in this lounge; you will add yours to this communal reservoir.

This is the porch and our garden.
Say hi to the jacaranda tree that makes its presence felt even in our garden.
I grow hardy plants here, most of them in pots. That fireplace needs fresh paint.
This garden is on the dull side – unlike that one at the Farmhouse B & B in Linden;
the garden you so loved because it reminded you of your home in Midrand.
Azaleas, marigolds, roses and lilies that I watched you cup in your hands and talk to:
I have these too in my garden. And these. Oh, and these as well. Look at these.
Come closer so we can listen to these pale purple petals as they land on the ground.

Speaking of hearts

It is hard to drag a painful heart everywhere she goes
so she packs it in the drawer where she keeps her underwear
to comfort it with the warmth of intimacy.

Then she goes out with a friend; they watch a movie, have dinner.
When her friend asks, 'How is your heart?'
She answers, 'Resting awash with memories.'

Like this horse

At the entrance to the Vodacom World building in Midrand,
just behind the massive swivel door,
stands a horse, fashioned from old cell phones;
a gigantic work of art whose message is clear
and overstated in writing: Recycle, Reduce, Re-use

Slightly shiny and pitch black,
front legs up in the air, bent
ready for a high jump,
head tilted to the back, focused forward,
hind legs firm on the ground,
each cell phone nestles with ease.

From a distance the eye doesn't
isolate the individual phones.
There is unity, grace, in this sculpture.
For my next lover I want to be like this horse;
distinct, strong, ready to jump with poise
into embracing arms of passion;
all my recycled parts together as one.

Touch

They ought to know not to be so loud in a book store –
particularly when I am working hard on Ben Okri
who demands more from me than any writer should.
They laugh louder than they speak – a youthful jollity.
Tempted to throw a nasty look in their direction,
I pause. The tone of their laughter makes me curious.
I stand, walk towards them and, start suspecting
these two are going to be together tonight, naked.

The bookstore's bright red fake leather couches touch
their guarded knees, almost touch my secret eye
that sees invisible rods connecting their irises.
He carries the 'Durban Indian,' look I learned about in childhood:
dark as 95% cocoa chocolate. His hands dance as he speaks
while his elbows nest where his thighs meet his torso.
To his left, the shelves of fiction authors, B to G, stretch;
anyone willing to see can tell: something is unfolding.

The other has the African Biography shelves to his right;
pale pink and unmistakably 'white', he talks more, and louder:
'Honesty is important to me and that's my truth.'
The window behind them speaks the city's language,
imminent winter darkness whispers a chilling breeze;
his words land on the other's moist receiving smile.
I want to interrupt with the words: young men, touch!
It already looks like you'll be naked together tonight.

To be Young, Lesbian and Black

Imagine being white, male and gay like the honourable judge!

People would treat me with respect, even before I speak;
they would invite me to meetings and listen to what I say,
quote my words and share them in various media,
publish my biography and the world would read it.

Imagine being white, male and gay like the honourable judge!

I am young, lesbian and Black like my murdered sisters.
I will never be white, male and gay like the honourable judge
who lives on the pedestal of public approval,
his sexuality flaunted on his behalf

while I live in the underground of collective disapproval,
my sexuality hidden on my behalf.

Chasing

When the sun sets I watch you stare
at clouds as they gather around it;
you marvel at how it touches sides with wonder.
As it dips behind the horizon,
bows a silent welcome to the stars and the moon,
holding your pain in the dark,
you continue to chase laughter.

It shouldn't matter

that I haven't brushed my teeth
when I talk to you on the phone, across the ocean,
from an island of mountains so blue and mysterious
I want to uproot and take back home. And really,
it shouldn't matter that my voice has morning hoarseness,
that my mind is still so foggy I cannot gather my thoughts,
that my tongue and lips are still lame and I cannot put words
together well,
that I still haven't showered so I could feel fresh and clean,
that I still haven't dressed up for the day to feel beautiful for us.

None of this should matter.

But it does.

Dance with me

What would it take
for you to dance with me –
high up, care free, spectacular?

What would it take
for you to fly with me –
behind me, somewhere, breath taking?

What would it take
for you to stay with me –
close by, everyday, intimate?

Counting Trees in July

Looking through a glass wall, I sit facing the south eastern direction,
counting trees whose names I do not know, bar the willow.
All of them are on the other side of the M1 highway – three lanes to
the north and three to the south. This is where the M1 gives birth
to the 11th Avenue and the Joe Slovo off ramps: the former facing
north, the latter south. However, the road sign encourages Joe Slovo
to remember it was once called the Houghton off ramp. These trees
stretch from the fence bordering the highway up to the suburb of
Houghton's hill where grand looking houses display their opulence.

But it's the billboard over the bridge that catches my eye:

> The first bank to offer iPads
> Now offers
> Generations

There is something wrong with that, I think, because iPads
have nothing to do with this soapie that audiences watch with
excitement. But maybe if I watched it I would know so I do need
to keep my mind from meandering into things unknown when I
should be placing my order and not irritating this waiter whose
name tag reads Imagination. If I wasn't busy counting trees I would
be a little friendlier. Every name has a story, this much we know.

But I am counting trees even though I think it might be easier
to focus on the cars speeding away at one hundred and twenty
kilometres an hour. I do not remember checking the speed limit
on this stretch of highway but there is no reason it is different.
These are cars of varying colours although most of them are varying
shades of grey in shapes and sizes beyond counting. I spot one with
leopard décor and soon after another is showing off its zebra stripes.
This is becoming an M1 zoo.

Most of these trees are green although we sit in the thick of winter.
Yes, an unusual kind of winter because it rained two days ago.

These trees have been green throughout winter. This distraction
is unwelcome.

I see Munro Drive. There it is, in between trees up on the hill
and the Munro viewing site. I spot a tourist bus stopping, people
stepping outside to stand against the rail and look
at the Johannesburg I call home.

After flying through the clouds while the ocean below waves,
I find the city you call home although I am still in Killarney
at Mugg and Bean, counting trees. The poem "Some of the
women" by Yvette Christiansë boldly inhabits my brain, yet all I
remember is the way it ends:

"...Some of them sang
Bread of Heaven and baked it just as good and some
of them found each other like honey-driven birds."

Some of the roads are closed for security reasons because
Obama is in Kenya right now.

My eyes back to the bill board; reading properly this time, I learn
that the first bank to give Ipads now offers generators.
Ah, those! Of course we shed our loads all over the country
in this winter of 2015, trust the banks to be the first to take
advantage of that. I trusted Imagination to return with my
heated soup and I know had I been in his shoes I wouldn't be
smiling either.

Through the glass walls, across these eight lanes of road and
daytime of rushing cars, I am counting trees. When I lift my gaze
further and the ocean waves interfere with my counting, I think
I need to start again with the willow tree closest to the highway.
Then I remember that the South African Book Fair kicks off this
weekend at the Turbine Hall in Newtown, and it occurs to me
that I have no idea how the Atlantic ocean got its name.

Imagination interrupts my counting as he asks: are you ready for your main course, ma'am? He should know I am not because I am not done counting. So I pause, repeat the number 58 in my head as I page through the menu now, and again lift my gaze to take in the image of Houghton I keep in my head.

This month of July is no longer ours – Mandela owns it from beyond. Indeed,some streets were blocked after he died; I had to modify my walking route.

A truck branded "Living Leaves" stands out amidst the rushing traffic. Just as you do in the traffic that is my mind when all I wish for is the stillness of rocks and the freedom of counting trees without any interruptions.

My jazz

This is jazz
Simple yet mystical

It's the jazz of my childhood
The razzamatazz of wonder

It's the cadence of youth
The gentle melting into adulthood

This is the jazz of womanhood
Deep & mellow against the wall of certainty

This is the jazz of middle age
Always piecing together like a quilt
Colours, shapes, positions, meeting points

This is my jazz.

The muffin-top moon

It is an hour before midnight.
Braamfontein is ready to sleep;
Silence has settled.

A few cars await their owners.
Street lights compete with
The muffin-top moon.

And as I close the door, a question beams
Into my mind: what shape will the moon be
When it rises on your side of the ocean?

Not yet Uhuru

The hazy silhouettes soon to
publicly express;
The mind recalls & lists the insults
publicly hurled;
The sudden release of a lover's hand
publicly held;
The body anticipates the onslaught
publicly executed.

The inaudible scream;
The paralysis;
The Letta song:
Not yet Uhuru.

At the Cumin and Coriander Restaurant

"Sir, I said no candles please."
The waiter looks at her then at the man next to her,
Who looks up: "You heard her, Bro. She said no candles, please!"
"It's the C & C protocol, sir, restaurant protocol," says the waiter.
"Are you telling me customers have no say?" the man asks.

The woman stands up slowly, pushes her chair farther back,
Adjusts her dress, snuffs out the light of both candles with one blow,
Clears her throat & starts addressing him in a well-practiced,
Controlled-and-loud-enough-for-all-to-hear voice:
"Mr. Waiter Sir, I have requested you three times already: NO CANDLES PLEASE!"
And follows with a lecture.

The diners at Cumin and Coriander listen, some with food in their mouths.
Some reposition themselves on their chairs,
Others who are becoming familiar with this look of a black professional woman,
Put their utensils down, sit up and listen. Between her words, you
Could hear a grain of rice drop. She ends with a question, asked slowly:

　　"So, please tell me, dear diners,
　　How many of you know what it is like to study
　　For four degrees . . . using the light of a candle?"

This

1

He was smiling.

There was fire
in the space
between your frames.

You were blazing.

2

Now that we know the texture
of each other's finger nails,
have seen the dirt find a home,
shall we call *this,* by its name?

Lunch

We started with carrot & sweet potato soup
Served with three sprinkling options:
Fresh coriander or sour cream or sunflower seeds,
Accompanied by a loaf of basil and beer bread.

Then there was a range for the main dishes:

A pan fried kingklip coated with flax seeds
Served on a flat rectangular wooden plate.

A three layer rice cake:
The bottom layer of brown and black rice with poppy seeds,
The middle layer of baby spinach, kale and parsley,
The top layer of pink salmon and parmesan cheese
Served in that star-shaped pine board.

Then purple cabbage cooked in port, red wine vinegar
With raisins, cubed pieces of pears flavoured with star anise
Served in the oval see-through, glass bowl which opens like a flower petal.

I made sure that our song played discreetly, on repeat.
But you didn't call, come, or answer your phone.

I did not move your chair away from the table.

The guests kept asking if you were still coming.

No, never

No. She never thinks of you
When she goes to sleep at night.
She never has a reason to.

She never thinks of you
even when her fingers
are on the Google search button.

She never thinks of you
when she hears your name being called.
She does not turn around with curiosity
to see who shares your once magical name.
Your face does not replace the stranger's face.

Not even when someone mentions your country
does she locate you in your home town with precision.
She packed everything away; she does not even remember
where things are. She wouldn't find them if she looked.

See, she never thinks of you
beyond answering questions when friends ask.
Then instantly she wipes you out of her mind.
No.   Never.   She no longer thinks of you.

Meeting point

Shall I sing a song of gratitude to Cato Manor
(Politics of the time and geography notwithstanding)
Or should I share the voices speaking of him years later?

1.

She says listening to 'Meeting point'
Is like peeling off the skin from her body
With a smile – then crying tears of fresh milk.

2.

Listening to 'Meeting point' makes him ready for death
Because his soul will cross over in orchestral harmony –
His hands clapping, feet stomping, laughter thundering.

3.

She says she stopped listening to 'Meeting point'
Because each time she did she started speaking in tongues and
She is afraid to find out what lies beyond that foreign fence.

4.

He says listening to 'Meeting point' is like
Hearing the sounds of a double rainbow, then
Walking, with eyes closed, into its embracing rays.

5.

She says listening to Sipho's 'Meeting point'
Is listening to a reincarnation of herself because
She and Sipho owned the oneness of otherworldly twins.

6.

Both said they only began to understand their reason for being alive
After listening together to Sipho Gumede's 'Meeting point'.
They never needed to listen to it again, ever.

7.

She says listening to 'Meeting point' is like listening to a prayer.
Whenever she needs to pray she turns on this song and goes on her
knees;
Its music is so much better than her sinful vocal renditions.

8.

'Meeting point' takes me to the waters of a massive lake
Next to which thousands of flamingos look like an earthly wave
Throwing its shadow onto the pink waters, said an octogenarian

9.

They say Sipho is their gift from Mvelinqangi
And the Mpangazitha ancestors, therefore all his music
Is theirs too – they never single out 'Meeting point'.

I will sing a song of gratitude to Cato Manor.
Even if none of them care to listen. I will tell them
That Sipho Gumede always knew what we all needed.

Isisu somhambi asingakanani, singangenso yenyoni
(For Mark Guy Foster)

Turn right when you should be turning left;
Ask for minutes when you should be asking for airtime.
But none of that matters because we laugh out loud,
Talk into the night, in the car: analyze, criticize and marvel together –
After all, this could be your other home.

I will search for keys in my handbag, find them after ten minutes;
Park the car askew, when the clearly marked white lines are straight.
But none of that matters because we dine out, wowed,
Talk literature, families and politics: analyze, criticize and marvel together –
During your visit to your other home.

Turn right when you should be turning left;
I will search for keys in my handbag, find them after ten minutes.
But none of that will matter because now we are aware
Of how special it is that we cannot undo our experiences together –
After all, this is your second home.

We mirror each other – what I see when you say that is Us:
Standing face to face, hands firm on each other's shoulders,
Feet touch, toe to toe, pupils piercing,
Chests beat in sync as if rehearsed for decades.
I wonder: have we been here before?

Ask for minutes when you should be asking for airtime.
I will park the car askew when the clearly marked white lines are straight.
It matters that we connected: held hands, walked streets, breathed the Jozi air,
Talked, read, ate and listened to poetry: analyzed, criticized and marveled together
In this South Africa that is now your second home.

Conscience

Look up and talk to the sky for as long as you wish.
The sun will not show up just for you.

Remove the wax from your ears, sit in a quiet room.
The music will not fill the air just for you.

Lay down naked in the pouring rain and pray.
The water will not clean your conscience.

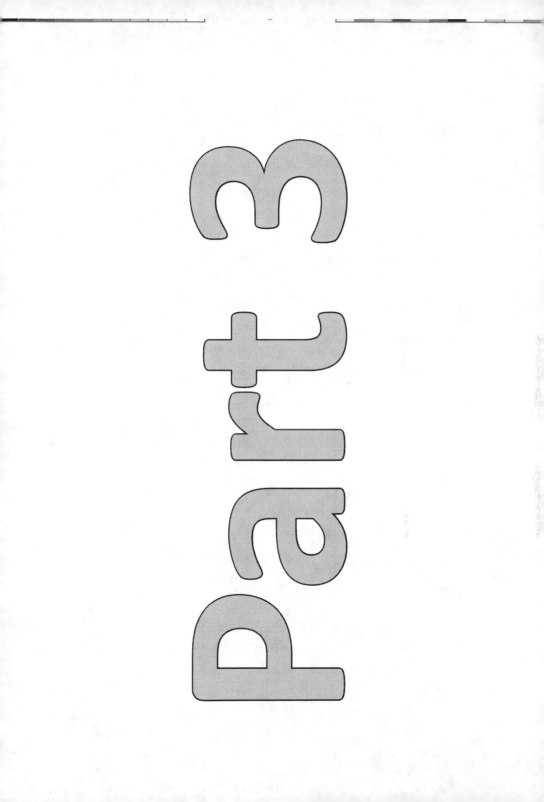

Part 3

Unfurling of the self

It began here: impalpably, without fear,
spectators and commentators.

Under Johannesburg's blanket of anonymity.

At my home of origin they ask
what happened to me. I answer . . .

Margins

On these margins I sew a hem,
tuck myself under, tack the fringe
then come out when I want
and dancing with one leg in the air,
one on the margin,
sing loud, generate rhythm.

When I tire, I breathe,
find my way through the stitches,
tuck myself under. Again.

My name is "Gentle Fingers"

When we woke up that morning,
Everyone had an errand to run –
It was the day of my sister's 50th birthday party.

But I, with Mama, almost alone in the house,
Hoped she would focus on me,
That she would call me by name.

I kept calling her, "Mama, mama!"
Wishing, hoping, dreaming, she might
Call me by name – at least once.

I walked her to the bathroom,
Washed her while she asked for directions
On what to do next.

Back in the bedroom,
I used my body cream
On her dry and creased skin.

Then she looked me in the eye, and smiled.
Without calling me by my name,
She said, "Yours are gentle fingers."

Black beret

When I wear my black beret, I often get comments
expressed in tones I am meant to read as compliments:

"Oh, you look like a real poet in that beret . . .
You could be walking the streets of Paris looking like that . . .
Hmm . . . that beret gives you an air of sophistication . . .
That Fifties look works well on you . . ."

I always smile, say thank you.

But what I really want to say is:
I wear this black beret when I miss my dead mother.

After the jazz

It is a quarter to midnight.
Home awaits in darkness.
When I turn on the lights, the mice
that have made my kitchen their home
will scurry away to hide.
So will the cockroaches.

Before I put the kettle on,
I will rinse it, drowning all the black ants
that have made its interior their refuge.
I will watch all the other ants
as they trek on into the cracks
on the wall behind while I wait.

From my bedroom, I will hear
the neighbour's dog barking; I will
trust that the neighbourhood is safe
with a dog so determined, a dog like that.
I will replay the music in my head:
the saxophone, the piano, the bass guitar – in harmony.

I hope to dream of the monkeys
I saw every day for two weeks in the grounds
of the Imperial Botanical Beach Hotel in Entebbe.
I hope to see them play in the trees with one another,
groom one another, run with their babies under their bellies –
Innumerable monkeys scratching, skipping, leaping.

The music in the background, a lullaby –
The saxophone, the piano, the bass guitar in measured ecstasy –
The monkeys chase one another towards the lake,
This tranquil lake of dark, rippling, night waters.
The smile on my sleeping face will last till morning
when an orchestra of birds sing me a wake-up.

Opening up like that

It is risky to open up like that!
What if something comes,
lodges inside the base of your petals
and irritates you?

It is dangerous to open up like that!
What if something heavy lands
on the tips of your petal
and breaks you off?

It is admirable to open up like that!
When something finally arrives
to touch sides with your gentle petals
it will be one with you.

It is delightful to open up like that!
Every eye that catches
the vibrant colours of your petal
instantly grasps the depth of your beauty.

Mynahs and raindrops

When it rained the smell of dry earth
Rose, found its passage through my window,
Filled my nose with its spice; so I inhaled spring.

Three mynah birds found shelter on the burglar bars
Of my bedroom window; two sat, the third stood as if
To look out for the others.

I turned off the radio, put down my book,
Closed my eyes and
Listened
To the mynahs and raindrops
Landing on my roof.

This pain

Opening up to this pain might kill me;
Closing up against it has nearly killed me.

Somewhere deep inside a knot sits:
On some days it feels as if it is getting bigger,
On others it feels as if it is splintering.

Today I want to slit my gut and look.

Jacarandas

From this height, I see them all –
The sprawling city pops their heads everywhere.

Sometimes I think of them as mushrooms;
Other times I see them as umbrellas.

Each October they reappear; to my ears they awaken
The purple sounds of spring.

Chosen markings

At first, we baked them in our wombs.
We vomited to ensure they were in the clear.
We burst into shiny girth circumferences,
Crisscrossed and creviced, just to make enough room –
We picked and we chose what went into our mouths.

Then we baked them in our arms, on our backs and breasts;
Skin to skin, eye to eye, wiping off excretions from their bodies.
And called their names so they could get used to them
just as we, too, had to. These names - our chosen markings –
live with them till this day:
Nala, Gugulethu, Phindile and Mpumelelo – names
With which to strut in the world.

Three women

Three women step out of the Calabash hotel.
A sudden wave of raindrop-filled wind
Hits them. They hug in haste, run to the cars;
Midnight approaches, sounding louder & louder.

In the black Mercedes Benz, the oldest woman
Turns on the heater before they take off.
They see the stories of Grahamstown in the architecture
Of buildings as they drive out of town.

The younger of the two, the driver of the Benz,
Steadies the car on the road while her mind jolts,
Crosses over, skips, stretches, scatters & returns
To the single holding thread: the warmth of sisterhood.

The oldest woman runs into her B & B on Harry Street
After saying goodbye, goodnight, thank you for everything.
In her room, she turns on the heater, the electric blanket,
The kettle & the ultimate dream: a world of women of wisdom.

The youngest, alone in her car, smiles
Unstoppably, to herself, as she drives into the night;
The voices of the two women still alive in her head.
In bed, her smile becomes the conductor of her dreams.

Paint brushes

We arrive in all our shapes and sizes,
Connect in many languages.

For clarity and emphasis
We use our hands and other body parts.
And when we disagree, we remind ourselves that
Our continent comes in many more colours
Than those of a rainbow and that
Our womanly ideas are paint brushes.

Namibia, we offer you our artwork-selves.

Secure in comfort

A is for amphitheatre.
C is for cattle kraal as well as chicken run.
V is for visitors' centre.
S is for swimming pool.

A is for all of us in the amphitheatre; some applauding, others
appalled.
C is for calling for cattle, chickening out & chanting away.
C is also for conviviality.
V is for visitors we would want to make comfortable.

Comfort while listening
To the sounds of cattle and chickens
Next to the swimming pool.
Secure.

The flow of fingers

They said, this is not just a painting, it is art.
They said this is not art, it is wall mathematics.
They said this is not wall mathematics, it is just a mural.
They said it is not just a mural, it is blazing beauty on a wall.

We agreed that we needed an apt word to capture this unknown
world.

She said: I move with the flow of my fingers, listen to the music
of the wall.

We have found a home for your cats
(For Gerald Vincent Kraak)

"Do not call before nine-thirty," you used to say.
But we knew what you really meant was: do not call before
midday.

"It's that time of year again," –
That's how your birthday party invitations often began.

A consummate host, a gourmet cook, a bottle of wine or whisky
at your side,
You gave love; you made laughter.

On the walls of your lounge pictures of handsome men,
Posters of activism, books of the universe, music of the heart.
Your foresight did not end with insights,
In your world, dreams do become reality.

And today we'd like you to know:
We have found a home for your cats.

Sorting

He approaches – coffee in hand, a smile on his face.
He puts the mug on the bedside table
Then he bends over to help me sort out
The varied miniature containers holding:

Folding toothbrushes of many colours;
Single use tooth paste tubes;
Ear muffs, eye covers, hand cream;
Miniature pens, notebooks, pairs of socks,
Moisturisers and a selection of haberdashery.

We put these objects in groups
And throw away empty containers.
We count the groups and items in each group
And place them in order on his bed.

This is taking a lot of time.

We smile wordlessly, thinking:
How can one accumulate so many
of these miniature things
That they need so much sorting?

The same smile is on my face
When I open my eyes and realize
It is the twenty-third day after his death.

Until you return

Your bedroom door begins the journey.
Ten doors later, one floor down,
We step out of Raymont Hall.

Our feet land on Wickham Street –
You, in your yellow walking takkies,
Me, in my cream Clarkes shoes.

On sidewalks with black and green rubbish bins
Placed outside these dark brown brick walls of homes,
Where people walk past you without ever greeting,

We head to Brockley station, tap our Oyster cards
at the turnstiles and walk through.
This is Lewisham, our temporary abode.

We write another chapter of our lives:
You, the child who is no longer a child;
Me, the person whose womb you chose.

I am back home now, to discover that
This is how my heart holds you these days,
Through London's July heat; until you return.

In your silence

The world has taken my words
Yet my story with you remains.
So I recite it in silence, in punctuation marks,
In my mind, alone, so I can keep it alive.

Here is my story, summarized:

It begins with a few question marks,
Continues through obvious exclamation marks,
A colon, followed by comma after comma –
Innumerable dizzying commas – so I breathe.

Later a dash, ushering unreadable words.
I know these world-renowned words,
But now they are unreadable, unutterable.
Another dash follows, in a river-like flow.

Then a question mark returns, a bigger one,
Then a space, a yawning space.
And, finally, a bellowing exclamation mark
followed by a very full stop.

Acknowledgements

"To be Young, Lesbian and Black" was inspired by Nina Simone's rendition of the song, *To be Young, Gifted and Black* a song I first heard in my youth and I embraced fully the message of promise it offered. This song helped me hold onto my sanity during my early adulthood years.

"Not yet Uhuru" came from a double inspiration; Thomas Glave's essay "On the Difficulty of Confiding with Complete Love and Trust in Some Heterosexual 'Friends'" and the iconic Letta Mbulu's song, *Not yet Uhuru*.

"Meeting Point" was inspired by Sipho Gumede's song, Meeting point. My sister Nomvula Radebe introduced me to Sipho's music.

"Chosen Markings" was inspired by a dinner with my daughter and nieces at Cafe Ganesh, Observatory, Cape Town on 27 September 2012.

"We have found a home for your cats" was written in in response to members of my writing group Christa Kuljian and Erica Emdon who suggested I write a tribute poem to Gerald Kraak (1956 – 2014) upon his death. I read the poem, "We have found a home for your cats" at a memorial event held in his honour at the Wits School of Public Health. I worked with Gerald for 3 years (2008 – 2010) at the Atlantic Philanthropies and as a consultant, leading the operationalisation of the Pilot Grantmaking Programme of The Other Foundation in 2013. We were in the same writing group when Gerald died. Gerald, may you rest in eternal peace.

On previously published poems

Some of the poems in this collection were previously published – some in earlier versions – in anthologies listed below.

• "Welcome" first appeared in *Scrutiny 2 Issues in English Studies in Southern Africa.* Volume 16, Issue 2 , 2011, with the mistaken title "Kitchen".

• "Speaking of hearts", "Sorting" and "My name is 'Gentle Fingers'" first appeared in, *No Serenity here. An Anthology of African Poetry in Amharic, English, French, Arabic and Portuguese* edited by Phillippa Yaa de Villiers, Isabel Ferrin-Aguirre and Xiao Kaiyi, 2010.

• "In your silence" first appeared in the Atlanta Review. South Africa: Women Poets edited by Phillippa Yaa de Villiers. "Three women" first appeared in Meridians: feminisms, race, transnationalism. AFRICAN FEMINISMS: Cartographies for the 21st Century Volume 17 Number 2 November 2018. Duke University Press. Edited by Ginetta E.B. Candelania, Alicia C. Decker and Gabeba Baderoon.

 • "Dance with me", "Opening up like that" and "My jazz" first appeared in, *Colours of South Africa,* Alex Fan Monis, The Expedition Project, 2012
"After the jazz" (26.11.2013) first appeared in, *Stray Anthology: An anthology of animal and poetry and stories.* Helen Moffett and Diane Awerbuck (Eds) Hands-On books, 2015

• "The sky agrees", Twenty-one houses" and "The nation was preoccupied" (then entitled "Shall we laugh?") first appeared in Illuminations. *An International Magazine for Contemporary Writing. Special South African* Issue 32. Summer 2017 Edited by Kobus Moolman.

•"At the Cumin and Coriander restaurant" first appeared in New Coin, Volume 53, Issue Number 1 June 2017 Edited by Dashen Naicker.

Words of gratitude

My sincere gratitude goes to Myesha Jenkins – a sister, poet, friend for reading the draft manuscript twice and giving me the needed feedback with the passion of a true poet.
Thanks also go to Dr. Barbara Boswell who read and gave me feedback and specific suggestions on some of the poems.

Thank you to the editor Allan Kolski Horwitz for engaging with the manuscript with such care and making such great suggestions. Thank you to the rest of the Botsotso team.

Printed in the United States
By Bookmasters